Miniature Fairy Gardens 101

A Quick Step by Step Guide on How to Make Your Own Fun Miniature Fairy Gardens

HowExpert Press & Casey Anderson

Copyright www.HowExpert.com

Recommended Resources

www.HowExpert.com – Short 'how to' guides on unique topics by everyday experts.

www.HowExpert.com/writers - Write About Your #1 Passion/Knowledge/Experience!

www.HowExpert.com/service - We Can Help Self Publish Your Own Dream Book!

www.HowExpert.com/gardening - Additional resource for Gardening enthusiasts!

COPYRIGHT, LEGAL NOTICE AND DISCLAIMER:
COPYRIGHT © BY HOWEXPERT.COM. ALL RIGHTS RESERVED WORLDWIDE. NO PART OF THIS PUBLICATION MAY BE REPRODUCED IN ANY FORM OR BY ANY MEANS, INCLUDING SCANNING, PHOTOCOPYING, OR OTHERWISE WITHOUT PRIOR WRITTEN PERMISSION OF THE COPYRIGHT HOLDER.

DISCLAIMER AND TERMS OF USE: PLEASE NOTE THAT MUCH OF THIS PUBLICATION IS BASED ON PERSONAL EXPERIENCE AND ANECDOTAL EVIDENCE. ALTHOUGH THE AUTHOR AND PUBLISHER HAVE MADE EVERY REASONABLE ATTEMPT TO ACHIEVE COMPLETE ACCURACY OF THE CONTENT IN THIS GUIDE, THEY ASSUME NO RESPONSIBILITY FOR ERRORS OR OMISSIONS. ALSO, YOU SHOULD USE THIS INFORMATION AS YOU SEE FIT, AND AT YOUR OWN RISK. YOUR PARTICULAR SITUATION MAY NOT BE EXACTLY SUITED TO THE EXAMPLES ILLUSTRATED HERE; IN FACT, IT'S LIKELY THAT THEY WON'T BE THE SAME, AND YOU SHOULD ADJUST YOUR USE OF THE INFORMATION AND RECOMMENDATIONS ACCORDINGLY.

THE AUTHOR AND PUBLISHER DO NOT WARRANT THE PERFORMANCE, EFFECTIVENESS OR APPLICABILITY OF ANY SITES LISTED OR LINKED TO IN THIS BOOK. ALL LINKS ARE FOR INFORMATION PURPOSES ONLY AND ARE NOT WARRANTED FOR CONTENT, ACCURACY OR ANY OTHER IMPLIED OR EXPLICIT PURPOSE.

ANY TRADEMARKS, SERVICE MARKS, PRODUCT NAMES OR NAMED FEATURES ARE ASSUMED TO BE THE PROPERTY OF THEIR RESPECTIVE OWNERS, AND ARE USED ONLY FOR REFERENCE. THERE IS NO IMPLIED ENDORSEMENT IF WE USE ONE OF THESE TERMS.

NO PART OF THIS BOOK MAY BE REPRODUCED, STORED IN A RETRIEVAL SYSTEM, OR TRANSMITTED BY ANY OTHER MEANS: ELECTRONIC, MECHANICAL, PHOTOCOPYING, RECORDING, OR OTHERWISE, WITHOUT THE PRIOR WRITTEN PERMISSION OF THE AUTHOR.

ANY VIOLATION BY STEALING THIS BOOK OR DOWNLOADING OR SHARING IT ILLEGALLY WILL BE PROSECUTED BY LAWYERS TO THE FULLEST EXTENT. THIS PUBLICATION IS PROTECTED UNDER THE US COPYRIGHT ACT OF 1976 AND ALL OTHER APPLICABLE INTERNATIONAL, FEDERAL, STATE AND LOCAL LAWS AND ALL RIGHTS ARE RESERVED, INCLUDING RESALE RIGHTS: YOU ARE NOT ALLOWED TO GIVE OR SELL THIS GUIDE TO ANYONE ELSE.

THIS PUBLICATION IS DESIGNED TO PROVIDE ACCURATE AND AUTHORITATIVE INFORMATION WITH REGARD TO THE SUBJECT MATTER COVERED. IT IS SOLD WITH THE UNDERSTANDING THAT THE AUTHORS AND PUBLISHERS ARE NOT ENGAGED IN RENDERING LEGAL, FINANCIAL, OR OTHER PROFESSIONAL ADVICE. LAWS AND PRACTICES OFTEN VARY FROM STATE TO STATE AND IF LEGAL OR OTHER EXPERT ASSISTANCE IS REQUIRED, THE SERVICES OF A PROFESSIONAL SHOULD BE SOUGHT. THE AUTHORS AND PUBLISHER SPECIFICALLY DISCLAIM ANY LIABILITY THAT IS INCURRED FROM THE USE OR APPLICATION OF THE CONTENTS OF THIS BOOK.

VISIT OUR WEBSITE AT HOWEXPERT.COM
COPYRIGHT BY HOWEXPERT.COM ALL RIGHTS RESERVED WORLDWIDE.

Table of Contents

Recommended Resources 2
Chapter 1: What is a Fairy Garden and why would I want one? 5
What Exactly IS a Fairy Garden? 5
What are they for? 6
Who are they for? 8
Chapter 2: How do I get started? 9
Choosing a Theme for your Fairy Garden 9
Choosing a Container for your Garden 11
Deciding if you want to build with others 13
Chapter 3: Buying Pieces for Fairy Gardens 15
Good Stores for Fairy Garden Materials 16
Don't Restrict Yourself to Garden Items 18
Watch Your Money! 19
Chapter 4: Found Fairy Garden Items 21
Everyday Household Items 21
Natural Pieces for Fairy Gardens 22
Other People's Junk 24
Chapter 5: Making Your Own Fairy Garden Pieces 27
You don't have to be Skilled 27
Useful Materials and Items 28
Useless Without Imagination 29
Chapter 6: Picking Your Plants 35
Remember your Theme, Plan your Plants 35
Finding and Purchasing Plants 37
Choosing Appropriate Plants 39
Chapter 7: Assembling and Planting your Garden 40
Gather All Items 40
Layout and Make Sure Everything Fits 41
Plant and Place 42
Chapter 7: Displaying Your Fairy Garden 44
Pick Your Location 44
Come Up with Your Fairy Story 45
Upkeep and Care 47
About The Expert: 49
Recommended Resources 49

Chapter 1: What is a Fairy Garden and why would I want one?

What Exactly IS a Fairy Garden?

Fairy gardens are a kind of limitless arena to use your creativity, green thumb, and even organizational skills. What's great about it is that you don't have to be particularly skilled at all. It's something you do for fun!

So a typical fairy garden consists of a container with dirt, a variety of plants (typically real but can be artificial), a structure of some kind for the fairies, and various other fairy sized items. These can be items such as a table and chairs, a pond, a playground etc.

This is something you make, via planting, assembly etc. and enjoy. It can be done alone as an adult, or can be done with children. It's a fun way to get anyone into gardening. It's whatever you want it to be, so you can't really mess it up!

One thing to keep in mind, the word fairy is not as exclusive as some people tend to think. A lot of people picture stereotypically pretty skinny girls with wings and flowery dresses when they think fairies. That's great, and there are a lot of fairy gardens like that! But, keep in mind the realm of fairy extends far beyond those beautiful creatures.

Your garden can also be based off goblins, gremlins, elves, mermaids, gnomes, and even dragons. I'm sure there are even more things I haven't thought of. So, don't assume your fairy garden has to be happy and pretty. You can have a scary garden full of fire colored plants and dragons, maybe some swampy plants and goblins, or even a beach scene with mermaids and palm trees.

What are they for?

Well, they aren't exactly about the destination as much as they are about the journey, like many things. They are for fun, for enjoyment and for…whatever you want.

I find it a relaxing and satisfying hobby. It gets me away from a computer screen and shuts my mind off to all the noise of the outside world. Sometimes my "to do" pile gets so high that everything seems like an insurmountable task. For me, that's a good time to gather some items and plants and build a fairy garden! After I'm done I feel like I've created something, accomplished something, and worked off some of my negative energy. How can you be angry looking at adorable little plants and fairies?

I've also used it as a way to learn about new plants. I'm a novice gardener. I enjoy it but I lack experience and land. I do all my gardening in pots on my balcony. One day I hope to have a yard. So, in the meantime, I experiment with new kinds of plants in my fairy gardens to see how well they fair in my climate zone. I can also see if I'm up for the care they require.

But honestly, the biggest reason to do is just to have fun and put a little whimsy in your life. We spend so much time doing things that we have to do, tasks that are a means to an end, jobs that we keep just for the paycheck. It's great to sit down and do something that is entirely pointless in the way most people value time.

With no expectations you don't have to be nervous about how it will turn out. You just do fun things that put a smile on your face. And then you can share those things with others to make them smile too.

Kids love fairy gardens. This is a great thing. Getting a child's attention on something that doesn't have a screen or Wi-Fi capabilities can be a gift, to you and them. It's a great way to bond with a child in your life, and to introduce them to the world of nature and gardening.

Help them understand how if they plan and plot out the fairy garden, it can be a wonderful display exactly how they want it to be. They can fit the most things in it. Or, let them run wild and cram it full of fairies and mini farm animals and realize at the end, they only put in one plant. Either way they learn from the process and have fun doing it.

So, in summary, here is a list of a few things that Fairy Gardens are for:

1. Fun
2. Relaxing, clearing your mind
3. Learning about gardening
4. Teaching children (gardening, planning etc.)

5. Experimenting with nature
6. Grounding yourself

Who are they for?

The easy answer to this is anyone and everyone! The obvious answer is women. Fairy Gardens are definitely most popular among women and girls. One of the things I want to do is break that idea that fairy gardens are "girly." One of the reasons it's mostly women that do it is because that's who it's marketed to.

My mom would often build fairy gardens with my niece, and my nephew would look on interested. But he didn't want to build them because they were "for girls." That's where I got my first thought to build dragon and dinosaur fairy gardens. Since he had the idea that the fairies were for girls, but clearly seemed interested in arranging the gardens, I thought that would be a great idea. I set about building my first dinosaur garden, and sent the pics for my nephew to see. Next time I saw him I had a few dinosaurs for him to use in his own garden.

My mother and I may have got a bit obsessed with the fairy gardens. We posted so many pictures of them on social media that others started being interested as well. Our county fair is going to have a fairy garden exhibit section for the first time this year!

Chapter 2: How do I get started?

Choosing a Theme for your Fairy Garden

Now, you certainly don't have to choose a theme. But for me, that's part of the fun. Actually I may even have more fun dreaming up a theme and all the little pieces that come together for it than I do actually building the garden. It's a close call.

First is there some sort of magical world on your mind that you'd like to build? Maybe you always loved My Little Ponies or other similar things, if so you want to build a world of magic flying ponies. Maybe you like fire breathing dragons or pretty flower fairies? Great, bring it on!

You could want to build it based on scene, a beach, a hidden forest, a desert? Or perhaps you want to create a market scene or a day at the park? Think of things that make you happy and what kind of adorable miniature world will make you smile. That's the important thing.

Once you pick your theme you get to think about all the charming things that belong inside of it. That's when your creativity can really come out to play.

Let's go with a beach theme!

Do you want something on the water, or on the beach? If you're going on the water, you'll probably want something to act as boat. If you're on the beach then, do you want to just do some beach chairs or blankets? Do your fairies want to be playing with tiny buckets and shovels? My first beach theme was a beach house; I wanted my fairies to be on the beach every day, living the salt life. Also keep in mind, on the beach you could choose mermaids instead of regular fairies!

Once I had my theme here some of the things I needed to think about.

a. Where would they live? What kind of house did I want? Or did I want a sea cave?
b. If I wanted the ocean, how will I create it and the beach around it? (blue aquarium rock is my favorite "ocean."
c. Where do I want them to sit outside their house? Blankets, lounge chairs or just in the water? Maybe a picnic table?
d. Did my fairies have hobbies or jobs around them? Some ideas: sand toys, surf boards, maybe ocean animals that they are tending?
e. Did I want to add to the ambience around them with anything? Sand dunes, fences, reefs etc.?

Of course I was never so organized to make a list of these things, I just thought over the ideas in my head. It's a fun way to occupy your mind if you're doing boring tasks at work or around the house. This part can really be the most fun, especially if you like to think creatively!

Choosing a Container for your Garden

There are times that I first see a container, and then try to think of a fairy garden that would work well inside of it. Usually in that case the theme will be built around the container. But you can also pick a container based off the theme. Whatever works best for you!

Don't limit yourself just to flower pots. They can of course make wonderful fairy gardens, but I like to stretch the limits of my imagination and user different bases to build my fairy gardens.

Here are just a few of the other things myself or my friends and family have used in the past:

Old bird cages
Partially hollowed tree stumps
logs
old wicker chairs
baskets
Tupperware
foil pans
old toy wagons
mason jars (terrarium style)
boxes (expect them to deteriorate)
mugs and tea cups
wheel barrows
old bowls, take out containers etc.
large candy dish
and more

Once you learn to think outside of the box you can

visualize almost anything as a good base for a fairy garden! And of course you can always just build them right on the ground. And the flower pots work too! I especially like the ones that have various levels with the broken pots.

One thing you have to take into account with your container is drainage. Unless you are planning on a fairy pond with aquatic plants, you will need to have proper drainage in your pots. What is proper depends on the type of plants you tend to use, but I always err on the side of having more drainage than I think I need. You can always block it later.

Many of the containers I mentioned above do not come with holes. This can easily be fixed with a hammer and nail, or a drill if you've got one. I don't, and many times have just used the back of the hammer to push holes through. It works. You have to have holes in the bottom of your container, unless it is very deep and you have some excellent soil draining built up.

In addition to holes you also want to think about the kind of soil and what to put on the bottom of the pot to help keep the roots from getting water logged. They make various things you can buy and cut to fit; they are honestly way easier and work great.

But I've used a lot of different material, rocks are common but many say not the best choice. It also makes your pots very heavy! Cut up dish scrubbies work. You can buy light fake rocks. Or, what I've been using most of late, plastic water bottles.

I don't eat anything that grows in my fairy garden, and being as I drink out of them anyway I figure what difference does it make? Instead of just recycling them I crumble them up and line the bottom of a pot with them. It's lightweight and helps keeps roots out of the water.

Once you have your container prepared you move on to your next step:

Deciding if you want to build with others

Fairy gardening can be a solitary or group activity. There are benefits with each style. I typically build mine alone. I like to destress and totally lose myself in what I'm doing. That's not something I can do if I'm conversing with someone else.

However, I do enjoy experiencing them with other people. I like to show them off and talk about them. I will tell everyone the story or idea I was trying to convey. I will talk about the different kind of plants I used and where I got everything or how I made it.

Sharing them is part of the fun for me, even though I don't like to share the actual building of them. I think because when my life feels chaotic I like the idea of doing something completely within my control. I can decide, dictate and do everything exactly the way I want it. Even when you're not a "control freak" type person this can sometimes be refreshing.

On the other hand, it can be really fun to share the building with someone. You can go through the whole process together if you want. You can plan, shop, and build all the pieces together, and then come together to plant and assemble the gardens.

It can be a one on one thing with a friend or get a whole group of people together to do it. You can share each other's pieces too. Some of the fairy items you buy come in packs of several at once so you can spread out the cost and have more unique items in your garden.

I love to show people and give them pointers on how to do different things. I love to help expose them to different perspectives and ways at looking at things related to fairy gardens. Hence me writing this book!

You can also do what I mentioned earlier and share the experience with children. This can be a lot of fun, but you need to let go of any expectation of structure. Let the kids have fun their own way. This is not usually a relaxing activity, but an enjoyable one.

So, if I want to destress and zone out, I'm not inviting kids to help me make a fairy garden. But if I just want to play and have fun, or spend some time with one of my nieces or nephews than it's a great idea. I do like getting them involved in nature and planting, as well as the imagination part of the fairy creatures.

Chapter 3: Buying Pieces for Fairy Gardens

The quickest and easiest way to get into fairy gardening is buying the various adorable miniature items that can be used inside them. There are of course lots of things you can make, and lots of fun to be had there, but I'll talk about that later.

Buying is what first interested me. I saw a few charming little houses and mischievous looking fairies. They were so cute; I just had to have them. But, what was I going to do with them? Of course at this time I had heard of fairy gardens, but not having a yard of my own I didn't think I could do them.

So, for months I'd stop by the little miniature fairy section of the craft stores and gaze longingly at the precious tiny items. Eventually, my girlfriend took notice. She decided to get a pretty box and fill it up with fairy garden items for me as a Christmas present. Little did she know the obsession she would unleash!

I made that first garden in an old pot with no drainage. It was all I had. She provided everything else, the house, the fairies, decorations and even plants. I spent hours planting, arranging, rearranging, designing miniature landscapes etc. I fell in love with it. So, I continued of course, and figured out some of the best places to get fairy items.

Good Stores for Fairy Garden Materials

The first and most plentiful are craft stores. In my area that consists of: Pat Catan's, Michael's and Jo-Ann Fabrics. Each of them offers some of the same brands and a few I can only find there. There are good points for all.

Jo-Ann's tends to be the most expensive, but they do have good sales. They also almost always have a decent selection of fairy garden things. Whereas the others tend to be more seasonal with only a few items found outside of spring/summer.

Michael's has the absolute cutest stuff usually. They also tend to have all the items for certain themes. For example last year they had a whole selection, everything I could imagine, for a summer carnival fairy garden. They had Ferris wheels, merry-go-rounds, roller coasters etc. There were also tiny ticket booths, food and game stands and other items. They tend to be mid-priced but have a great variety in season.

Pat Catan's is usually the cheapest. They don't have as large of a supply as Jo-Ann's, or as much themed items as Michael's, but they have really cute and affordable stuff. They have tons of great fairy houses and fairies. They tend to have less of the "extras."

The home improvement type stores also sometimes have a section devoted to fairy gardens. Lowe's has a decent one; Home Depot usually has a small shelf in the spring season. Their stuff tends to be over-priced, but sometimes you get lucky.

Random stores, like discount stores, have them off and on. Our local Big Lots has a whole row of fairy things in the summer and Christmas themed fairy things in the winter. They have great deals as well. Dollar Trees, Dollar Generals etc. will get stuff in on occasion. You should always keep an eye out.

There is also of course that wonderful place called the internet. There are lots of sites with loads of fairy gardening items. There's Amazon, which tends to have the decorated pots and kits more than individual items.

There's also Etsy. If you want something homemade, but not by you, this is the perfect place. Like anything else at Etsy the prices can be all over the place. Sometimes you'll find adorable tiny handmade table and chairs sets at a great price; other days you'll find someone charging $6 for 3 cotton balls they call sheep.

Another site that I know many people use is Wish (they also have an app). I've heard good and bad. Basically everything comes from China, it's dirt cheap, but it often takes a very long time to get to you. I've heard they have trouble with hackers, but I don't know anyone that's actually experienced that. I do know people who have gotten items from them and loved it. They have a ton of fairy garden related items. Many of them come in bundles, like for example you'll get 12 tiny white bunnies, or 15 pieces of fence etc.

Don't Restrict Yourself to Garden Items

The first and easiest way to start collecting items for fairy gardens is to buy the kind of things that are marketed for that purpose. But there are way more options than that. There a lot of store bought items having nothing to do with gardening that make for great fairy garden accoutrements.

One such thing is toys. Tiny toys are all the rage right now. Just about every popular franchise has some sort of mini mystery package. Disney has a lot of those little Squinkie things of various characters that can be used. There are Shopkins, different kinds of trolls, My Little Ponies and more. I like to use the Disney Fairies (Tinkerbell & Co) Squinkies, as well as Lalaloopsy. They also can come with small houses, pets, accessories etc. that you can use in your gardens.

If you have kids, or know someone who does, you can usually find many of these kinds of toys discarded. Or the parents are eager to be rid of them and the child no longer plays with them. There are also the little quarter machine toys. Many of those will work in a fairy garden. Locally there are a lot of the machines with tiny ninja characters. You could make a great miniature ninja garden.

You can also always use the little mini bags of toy soldiers, dinosaurs, reptiles etc. that you can find. Once you start looking around the toy section you will see that there are tons of options. And they can be quite cheap! Check the dollar stores too!

Tea cups are another favorite for many to use for fairy gardens. They have to be SUPER tiny gardens, but they are darling. Now those are hit and miss with price. Sometimes you can find some cheap ones at places like Goodwill, other times they are like $50 apiece and "vintage."

Another favorite of mine is fish aquarium decorations. You can find those anywhere with pet supplies usually. There are little fake trees, rock formations, houses, dragons, Buddha statues, all kinds of things. Some look very fake and are hard to fit in, others fit perfectly in various fairy garden themes.

Watch Your Money!

This one is extremely important as well as extremely easy to forget. If you're like me, you just fall in love with all the tiny adorable things. You have a million ideas in your head and want to buy things for all of them. And sometimes you just see something that's so freaking cute, it doesn't fit with any of your themes but you just have to have it anyway!

It's great if you can do that. But, myself, I'm not independently wealthy. I'm guessing most of you aren't either. But I'd be lying if I said I never let myself get out of control. It certainly happens. But that just means that later I have to cut back on something, which isn't always a good thing.

One thing to do of course is look for sales. Go shopping at the end of season, or the off season. Save and look for coupons. Craft stores in particular produce lots of coupons. You have to read them carefully to see how they can apply, but sometimes you can save a ton.

One of the things I do to help control my spending is make a list before I go. As well as pick the theme that I am shopping for, and try really hard to stick with it. So, if I'm shopping for my Halloween fairy garden, I'm not even going to LOOK at the Christmas fairy shelf. I may however look at some of the clearance items. Ok I always look at the clearance items. Even though the houses, fairies, boats etc. never go bad, they do go out of style and season. Towards the end of summer all the flower and beach themed items will be getting marked down to make room for Halloween and Christmas. (I've never noticed Thanksgiving themes, but they do have general Fall themes.)

So, I'll try to only purchase items for my theme, unless they have something really cute on clearance of course! And I set a dollar amount before I even go to the store. That's a must. The pretty and well-made items like houses, table and chair sets and more tend to be pretty pricey. It's easy to forget that when they are so small and charming.

Also, never forget to hit up places like Goodwill, yard sales, etc.

So, this can be a very expensive hobby. BUT! It doesn't have to be. There are ways to have more frugal fairy garden fun! Read on!

Chapter 4: Found Fairy Garden Items

While buying things is a lot of fun, finding them can be just as exciting. And much less financially devastating! You can find them around the house, in nature and at other people's houses. All you need to do is look at everything with fairy garden eyes! Look at things while ignoring their typical functions. Think of everything from the eyes of something a few inches tall. Soon you will see all kinds of things in a new light!

Everyday Household Items

The first place to start is your own home. I started with looking at small, discarded things. For example, a few old golf tees. Their small, seems the perfect fairy size...what could I do with that? I wasn't sure yet, but I set them aside in my craft bins. Later I found a few spare marbles, not even sure where they came from. But, they are pretty and small.

So, I went to put them in the craft bin by the golf tees and oh! Fairy gazing balls! Glue the marble on to the top of the tee, stick in the ground and boom fairy gazing ball. You can paint the tee a pretty color or the marble too. I kept my first ones plain.

Ordered pizza...you know how sometimes they come with those weird little white plastic things in the center, with like 3 sticks and a flat top? I guess they are to keep the box from pressing on the cheese, but not sure. Anyway, what does that look like to you? To me, it's a perfect little fairy table.

Extra beads can make great little fairy baubles and decorations. Or if their small enough you can treat them as fairy gravel or mulch, and use them in the tiny gardens of your fairy gardens.

Once you open your mind to the possibilities you can find tons of things in your house to be used for fairy gardens. What could you do with some clothes pins? An old take out container? A broken picture frame?

Maybe you used to have a shot glass collection but you're not particularly attached to it anymore. Turn them over and you have fairy pedestals. Or leave them right side up and it becomes a fairy vase or bird bath.

Natural Pieces for Fairy Gardens

Nature is often the best place to look for fairy garden materials. A lot of people only want to go with natural products for their gardens. They gather and make all their decorations. I think that's great! I have done that as well, but usually do a mix of natural and manmade. I like the Tinkerbell style of fairy gardens, she was known for liking to use "found" objects that were man made in her house.

The options for natural pieces can be endless. Here's a list of some of my favorite and most commonly used:

Sea Shells
Driftwood
old logs & branches
dried moss
rocks
crystals (amethyst, quartz etc.)
dried and hollowed gourds
dried flowers
found feathers
dried seed pods
mud! (You can form it)
tree bark
sand
vines
acorns
Buckeyes

You get the idea right? Basically...anything. Now, what do you do with these acquired natural items? That depends on several things for one, the size of your fairies. If you are building for very small fairies, then dried milkweed pods make wonderful beds. You can even put some of the fluff in them.

If your fairy is slightly larger, than that same pod can be a chair or a decoration on their house, or a bed for a pet of theirs if you have a tiny cat or dog or other animal to go with them. Similar situation with the sea shells, some large ones can be used as beds, or even houses. Small ones could be tables or chairs, or just decorations.

You can build houses out of the bark, branches or driftwood. Or you can use very small pieces as fencing. Larger logs can be hollowed out a bit and turned into homes. Dried moss makes great flooring for any fairy home, or softness to add to the beds.

Rocks can be many things. They can just be decorations; they can be used as seats and tables. They also can be painted to look like houses. This is sometimes a cheap and easy way to build a fairy house, assuming you have paint and at least a little talent. Then your house can be as colorful or natural looking as you want. You can't paint it pink with purple shutters, or you can merely draw a door and windows, making it look like they just moved into the rock.

Gourds make amazing fairy houses. They can be hard to cut into, so you'll need some serrated and strong tools, but they can be great houses. Cut a door and a window or two. Line the bottom with moss or leaves. Set up some little furniture out of rocks, shells etc. Use feathers or dried flowers like curtains for the windows. You can also decorate the gourd with crystals. They add some natural sparkle to your fairy house.

Other People's Junk

This may seem like a strange section, but it's often the most frugal way to fairy garden. Especially if you aren't using all natural items. So, what am I talking about here? Well, mostly yard sales. And thrift stores, flea markets. Sometimes chain stores like Goodwill or The Salvation Army, other people are lucky enough to have some family owned thrift stores and second hand shops in their area.

The cheapest options are usually yard sales. Often people will sell things that are still in good condition and just no longer fit their lifestyle. One thing I have a lot of luck finding at yard sales is flower pots. Many people have a ton, and gardeners tend to get them as presents a lot and buy more than they have need of. You can use the flower pots both for building your fairy gardens in and the smaller ones can be made into fairy houses.

They also tend to sell a lot of knick-knacks, like little statues, decorative plates etc. Maybe this person used to love birds, and now they have 1000 little bird statues that they need to pare down. These could look very cute in a fairy garden.

One thing people sell a lot of is toys; children are constantly growing out of them. Well, little doll houses, cars, campers etc. also make great houses, cars and campers for fairies. Or maybe you can get a whole bin of Littlest Pet Shop or Army men for something like $1. Use these all around your fairy gardens.

Sometimes the quirkiest items can be turned into cute fairy garden material. I once found some old Avon lotion bottles shaped and painted like owls, they were like $0.25. I added them to a fairy garden I already had and they were the perfect size, like the fairies were made to fly on them. An old eye shadow palette makes a great fairy paint set. You can set up your fairy at some sort of canvas, for example a rock or a big leaf, with the eyeshadow set and a little brush, viola! Fairy Van Gogh!

Chapter 5: Making Your Own Fairy Garden Pieces

To be honest, this is something I love the idea of more than I love doing some times. It's awesome to make your own stuff! But sometimes it's a lot of work. However there are plenty of easier ways to do them as well that I've found. So, you can make it as simple or as complicated as you want. Your fairy garden can be as plain and natural or elegant as you'd like. If you're making the pieces you have total control over the ambiance of your fairy garden. Bringing me to my next section:

You don't have to be Skilled

You can absolutely make intricate and elaborate fairy garden houses, furniture etc. If the making is one of the parts you enjoy and are good at, then live it up! Buy fancy wood and metals, draw out a blue print and build an amazing fairy villa. It will be SO cool. But, maybe you want that but you don't have the skill or ambition? Well, maybe you are lucky and you have a friend or family member who is particularly talented in this area. Don't be afraid to ask, some people love to make gifts for others with their talent. Offer to buy the materials and help with the process. Maybe it's a good chance to bond with that Aunt, Uncle, and Cousin Etc. that you never get to see.

Let's say neither of those are an option. Guess what? That's totally okay! You don't' have to be exceptionally skilled to make your own fairy house or furniture. Honestly, all you really need is patience, imagination and the ability to acquire some building materials. And sometimes, patience isn't even required.

Useful Materials and Items

There are far too many for me to list them all. However, I'm going to list a few things that I've used.

Basics:

Modge Podge
Wood glue
Hot Glue gun
Tacky Glue (you get the idea right? Lots of glue variety)
Paint
Scissors
wood cutting utensil
tweezers (especially with small projects)
small nails sometimes

Additional items:

Terra cotta flower pots
colored gravel (like for fish tanks)
plain gravel
Bark
Popsicle sticks
Wood of various kids
Plastic bottles (2 liters, 2oz, juice bottles, laundry detergent bottles etc.)

old forks and spoons you don't mind losing
tea cups
empty butter bowls or other bowls
old plates
Old/broken wicker furniture
Old metal wire style shelfing
Disposable pie pans and cake pans
old Tupperware/Rubbermaid
colored craft pipe cleaners
colored vinyl or other semi waterproof style paper
buttons

You get the idea right? All kinds of things can be turned into exciting fairy garden material. You just need imagination! This leads to my next section!

Useless Without Imagination

Alright, so now you've gathered some of those and other material. You're excited to get started! But, you don't know just what you want to do with it all. Well, you really have to use your own imagination and decide what gets you excited to think about.

You should already have a theme and your starter container at this point. It's also easier if you've already purchased any additions to your garden you're going to want. Like a fairy.

I usually start with making a house for the fairy to live in. No, there doesn't have to be a house, it can be a fairy park, fairy patio, fairy carnival, whatever you want. But usually there is one main central "structure" to the garden. That's what I start with.

Let's say you are going to build your fairy house. You're not particularly worried about look natural, and want to go for bright and fun instead. Fantastic! Here are some instructions for building a house out of a 2 liter pop bottle.

Step One: Remove the label and cut off the top 1/3 of an empty 2 liter bottle as cleaning as possible. You should have one section that includes the neck and lid, and one that has the base of the bottle.

Step Two: Cut a wavy edge along the wide part of the top section making it seem to flair out. This will be the roof of your fairy house.

Step Three: Pick your colors and paint your bottle. If you want to go super bright and girly, try doing a purple roof with a pink house base. But, any colors you choose will work!

Step Four: Add any painting details. If you have one, use a paint pen to draw shingles on the roof. Paint some windows or decorations around the house.

Step Five: Decide where you want your door, and how. You can do a round bird house type door or a rectangular door fashioned off humans. Cut out your door.

Step Six: Glue your pieces together. Use your hot glue gun to add a line of glue all around the outside of the top of your base. Take the top part and lower it over the bottom until the inside of it lines up and sticks to the glue on the outside of the base. Let sit until dry.

Step Seven: Decorate your fairy house! You can glue dried flowers or fake flowers to the outside. You can glue buttons. You can use small leaves or feathers as curtains. Whatever you want! You can also decorate the inside a bit with moss or straw or some other flooring.

You've now built your own fairy house! And it could be almost entirely recycled materials if you wanted!! There are of course lots of other things you could do. You could glue together small branches, or Popsicle sticks into a house shape. You could cover a bottle in glue, roll it in gravel and make what appears to be a stone fairy house! Possibilities are endless! Of course, as I said, use your own imagination. I wanted to give you some ideas and a walk through to get you started though.

Here's another kick start for the imagination. You can make more than just houses. You can make all the furniture too. You can use wood, sticks or Popsicle sticks to make beds, tables, chairs etc.

How about a table out of sea shells? Sounds great right? It's perfect for a nice fairy (or mermaid) beach scene. Gather/purchase your shells, I find it's best to have one large somewhat flat shell, and 4 little shells all of similar shape and size. It doesn't have to be perfect.

Now, I like to flip the large shell upside down, so it seems kind of like a bowled table. The shell might not look as cool but it feels more realistic to me. But it will work either way!

Next take the 4 smaller shells and using your hot glue gun to glue them to either the outside (if it's bowl side up) or the inside of your larger shell. Hold them in place a few moments then let them dry. Make sure they all end evenly, so your table is not lopsided. Or you might want to leave it lopsided and build your garden around that. Perhaps you want to have a sand dune or a hill and have your table built into it. In that case you would want one leg a little shorter into the hill/dune.

Another cool thing you can build yourself is a waterfall. You have to be careful with this one as you can burn your fingers. But here's a cheap and easy way to build your own fairy waterfall.

You will need: Hot glue gun and glue sticks, small rocks, a thin strip of flexible plastic a little longer than you want your waterfall to be(even a piece of plastic zippy bag can work), a toothpick and any decorative features you may want. Like moss, a tiny fish etc. You also need a flat and preferably metal surface, something that will not be too hard to peel the glue off.

Step One: Make an oval on the metal surface as large as you want the "pool" of your waterfall to be. Let that harden a bit them make another circle inside of that.

Step Two: Once both outside ovals harden you want to fill in the circle entirely. Letting the outside harden first gives more texture to your pool. Don't worry if there appear to be bubbles, it looks natural as water. Leave the whole thing to harden.

Step Three: Carefully pry the hot glue circle off the metal surface; a sharp flat knife works best for this. You want to be careful not to break the glue, or hurt your fingers.

Step Four: Once you've released the glue circle you want to add your rocks around it. Place a small amount of glue at a time, then press down a rock. Line the whole edge of the pool with rocks. Let harden.

Step Five: Build up. Pick a section of the pool to build up the waterfall. You can cascade it over rocks like stairs, or you can just have it fall from the rocks. If you are building a falling waterfall make a small tower out of rocks while hot gluing them together. It works best if you make it stick out over the pond a little at the top.

Step Six: Take your small piece of flexible plastic and glue it to the top rock, hanging over the pond. Let that harden. Then bend the plastic down and glue the bottom to the pond below.

Step Seven: Run the glue up and down the plastic strip. This will be your waterfall. It does not need to be flat or perfectly even, water usually isn't. Make it as wide and thick as you think it needs to look realistic. Just make sure to have the glue follow from top to bottom.

Step Eight: Time to get your toothpick. If the glue at the base of the waterfall where it hits the pond is still a bit soft you can use your toothpick to poke at it and pull up. This makes it look like the water is splashing as it hits the bottom. If your glue has already dried just add a few dabs more and use them. Pull the glue in different directions so it looks like natural splashes.

Step Nine: Decorate around the pond as you see fit!

Now you've made your own miniature waterfall! How cool is that!? You can go as plain or elaborate as you want. You could use blue hot glue sticks to make it look more like water. Or you could paint the glue once you've done it. You can make it as large or small as you'd like. You can add several fall points, or add fish, or other wildlife drinking from the pond or waterfall. You can glue twigs to look like trees, whatever you'd like. Your only limit is your imagination!

I hope these ideas kick started your creative process! You don't have to do any of them. These are just some ideas to get you thinking about what you can do with items you have. Let that be the beginning of a bunch of DIY projects for your own fairy gardens!

Chapter 6: Picking Your Plants

Sometimes this feels like the most fun part! It can also sometimes be the most expensive, but it doesn't have to be. If you're like me, you can easily get carried away buying all the cute, adorable little plants. Try to set a budget for yourself, and get a smaller basket/cart so you can't fit too many! The best thing I've found, is to make a plan before you get to the greenhouse/store etc.

Remember your Theme, Plan your Plants

So, as I said, planning protects you from going overboard. Now, you may be able to grow your own plants, either indoors or in a greenhouse. In that case you'll have more control and opportunity when it comes to plants. But, that's not something I can do, so I'm going to talk about when you have to either purchase, or seek out plants.

At this point you should have your theme, and you should have the pieces you want to put in your fairy garden. Sometimes it's easiest to pick your plants in accordance with your theme. For example, if you have a desert theme then pick cactus plants, if you have a beach theme pick plants that look like palm trees or beach grass. You get the idea.

Of course you can just pick plants you like too. Pick what looks pretty/cool/scary, whatever you're going for. You might want to be aware of the size of your plants compared to your fairy house or fairies. You might want to do things to scale. You don't have to, but you do want to make sure that your awesome fairy house and anything you made does not get overshadowed by a giant plant.

Many of the miniature ground cover plants you find tend to spread quickly, so you may have to prune them throughout the season. A lot of the larger chain stores will have whole sections dedicated miniature/fairy plants. Check there! Here are some good plants for very gardens:

1. Polka Dot plant. This one is loved for its pink, red or white splatters on green leaves. It looks very enchanting. It will need pruned to not overgrow your fairy garden though.
2. Mexican Heather. This is a pretty, blooming shrub that can be kept small with pruning and you can shape it to look more like a fairy tree!
3. Sedum. So many kinds. They spread fast but cover nicely and often stay low to the ground. Some bloom.
4. Elfin Thyme or other kinds of thyme. Thyme tends to form think mats of plants and adds wildness to your garden. The Elfin kind gets covered in pink blooms. Lemon Thyme smells like lemons when rubbed. Look around at other thyme options.
5. Miniature Oakleaf Creeping Fig. Its small leaves are perfect for fairy gardens. It also has a rich green color.
6. Coleus. They can come in bright colors and make a nice scene in your fairy garden. You can prune back as it grows.

7. Ripple Peperomia. This petite plant comes in burgundy and green; it stays small and fits well.
8. Golden Monterey Cypress. With full sun it can have a bright gold color. It's like a fairy pine tree.
9. Baby tears. This adorable lime green looking plant is great.
10. Succulents. There's a wide variety of succulents that are great and well-draining fairy gardens.

That is by no means a comprehensive list. These were just a few to get you started!

Finding and Purchasing Plants

As mentioned before, a lot of stores will have sections dedicated to this and you can get your ideas there. Especially chain stores like Lowe's and Home Depot. But many Greenhouses will have tables set up for fairy gardens as well. If not, the workers at local green houses are almost always excited to talk to you and give you tips and guide you to the right plants.

If you can have an idea of what you want before you go shopping, all the better. You might be more successful at sticking to your budget that way.

If you have the option to trade or take plants from friends and family, definitely do that first. Many people who garden like to trade plants, it gets them something new to grow and see. Plus, there's always a joy in giving things to others!

With plants you know that they will see them nearly everyday day and think of you. It's fun to have a garden full of things you can tell people who they came from. So you can swap plants you have with ones they have you don't, or sometimes people just give you starters. I've also bought plants to share. Sometimes the low growing fairy plants come in bunches, and I only need one or two. See if someone wants to split them with you, you save money and don't waste plants.

Another great possibility is to find plants on your own out in the wild. This is especially good for mosses. You can find many beautiful varieties of moss in a wood. You just have to be careful where you gather.

Your own property is preferable, or that of a friend or family member who is ok with it. You cannot take from state parks, unless they are having an event to do so. Occasionally state parks will need to thin out various plants and ask the public for help. But never assume it is ok, you must always talk to a ranger and get permission.

Look under and around felled trees, as that is the perfect home for moss. When you find some, make sure not to take the whole thing, else you will kill the plant. Break off a small piece of bark, or hunk of plant from the earth. Make sure you rebury any roots you exposed.

Choosing Appropriate Plants

Not all plants can grow in all environments. It is important to know the proper care needed for the plants you choose. It is possible that for a short time a plant can grow in a poor environment if you are lucky. But, it's always best to prepare an appropriate one.

You need to know if your plant needs well-draining soil, lots of water, and little or full sun. Some plants work better with different kinds of soil, but typically most of what you can buy or find will work.

You want to know if the roots are likely to grown more down or out. This will help you planning the best pot and layout for your fairy garden.

No one does it perfect every time. If you don't have the exact recommended set up that does not mean your plants won't survive. You just want to give them their best chance.

Be careful not to mix cactus or plants that need little water with any plant that requires consistent watering. This is one of the biggest things. Keep like plants together.

Chapter 7: Assembling and Planting your Garden

Now for the best part! This is the part where you can get lost in a fantastic fairy world! Remember to take pictures! It adds to the fun and helps give you ideas for other fairy gardens. And you can show your friends and family. Several of mine enjoy fairy gardening as well and like to see what other people are doing.

Gather All Items

This might seem like a silly thing to say, but, you want to make sure you have all the pieces of your fairy garden with you when you start building. It makes things way easier. Basically that's:

1. Pot you are building garden in
2. Potting soil or dirt for planting
3. Plants
4. Drainage items (rocks, sand etc.)
5. Fairy house
6. Fairy decorations
7. Fairies
8. Gloves
9. Any planting tools
10. Water

Those are the basic things you will need. If everything is within reach it makes the planting go way easier. I also like to either sit in a chair or stand at a table, rather than kneeling on the ground. So, I recommend a set up like that if you can do it. Way better on your back!

Layout and Make Sure Everything Fits

You should have your basic plan in place now for your fairy garden layout. But, now that you have everything in front of you, you should place it into the pot. You want to make sure it all fits the way you imagined it.

Sometimes I find that I have a little less room in the pot than I thought or even a little more. That depends on what style you're looking for. Do you want an overgrown forested looking area for your fairies? Or do you want a trim looking yard?

That will help you decide how much to put into your fairy garden pot. Some people like more plants then fairy items, and some people want more houses and fairy furniture. It's up to you. You might not even be sure until you start to late it all out in the pot.

Sit the plants down on top of the dirt first, and place the fairy items around them. You want to look it over before you start digging and planting. The less you mess with the roots of the plants the better.

That doesn't mean you can't make any changes after you do it. I've dug up and replanted several plants from fairy gardens before. It's just easier if you can set it all up one time. Plus there's always a risk the plant won't bounce back after being repotted.

Plant and Place

Alright! Everything is laid out and planned now! Time to get your hands dirty! Hopefully this is something you enjoy! If you've never planted before, here are a few tips:

1. Wear gardening gloves. They keep your hands slightly cleaner, protected from any splinters, and if you come across any worms or bugs they don't touch your skin!
2. You need little garden shovels; hulking ditch digging equipment won't help you. You need a transplanting spade and a small hand rake particularly.
3. Wear a hat if you're out in the sun, shade your face and neck.
4. Remember to hydrate. It's easy to get distracted and forget to drink, make sure you have something with a lid nearby and visible to remind you.
5. Wear something you don't mind getting dirty.

Those are very basic planting tips for those that don't know. Now, you want to put the plants in first and then insert the fairy house and other items around them.

Most plants come with some instructions on the pot, telling you how deep, how much space etc. Follow that as closely as possible. Some of them will say things like "leave 6 inches of space between plants." This will not always be something you can do in a container garden. Those instructions are often assuming you want your plants to get large. If you want to keep them pruned it's ok to have them closer together.

You want to make sure not to hide any small plants behind large ones, unless of course, you're setting your fairy garden up to be viewed on all sides. Then you will have some smaller ones behind from some angles. Remember to layer things around the pot. You don't want all the plants shoved in one corner and all the fairy items in another.

Set up your fairies as if you are a child playing with dolls. Have fun with it. Play! Use your imagination. Have a fairy kneeling on the ground in front of a vegetable garden. Lie out a mermaid on the edge of your "water" and the sand. Have two fairies on a teeter-totter. You get the idea. You want to make it look alive.

Think about it this way, if a child comes across your fairy garden you want them to see it as a magical world. Do your best to make it look that way!

Chapter 7: Displaying Your Fairy Garden

You did it! You made a fairy garden! Hurray! I hope you had as much fun as I do. And you should be proud, you created something. Maybe it's not something huge, but you did create something. You used your imagination and your skill and your own hands and put together something beautiful, or adorable, or maybe even scary. You made it your own. Congratulations!

Pick Your Location

So, where are you going to put it? I wish I could put more in my house, but, the cats eat them. Granted that has made for some good Catzilla photo opportunities with the fairies and the cat, but I get pretty bummed if they ruin pieces. And even more upset if the cats get sick from eating plants.

So, that is something you have to consider. If you are bringing them inside, make sure they are out of reach of pets of children who may put pieces in their mouth. You also have to make sure your garden will get enough sun inside.

There are similar concerns for outdoors. If you have outdoor pets, or get visited by local raccoons, they may want to play in your fairy garden too. A friend of mine from work put together a beautiful fairy garden right on the ground near her house, it looked lovely.

The next day, raccoons had torn apart the whole thing and pieces were flung everywhere!

A lot of animals like to dig in fresh dirt. Sometimes having it in a container will help with that, or if it's raised off the ground. This might not be something you have to worry about at all though.

You want to display it for people to see, so don't hide it in a side yard no one ever goes to. Put it near or on your porch or patio. Make it a center piece of your outside entertainment area.

You want to see it as often as possible and you might want to show it off to others. I know I do! My family and some of my friends and I have a bit of a contest to see who can create the best fairy garden. So naturally we want to show them off as much as possible, it's part of our fun.

I also love to share pictures of my fairy gardens on Facebook. Since I have a group of people that enjoy doing it as well we like to look at pictures of each other's. You can always create a group via Facebook just for that. You want to enjoy what you do as much as possible, fairy gardens are no exceptions.

Come Up with Your Fairy Story

This might not be something you enjoy, but I like to create a story for my fairies. I'm a creative time and love reading and stories in general. So, often when I make a fairy garden I've created a background for all the fairy creatures. Obviously you don't' have to do this if it doesn't sound fun.

For example, I had one garden that was more elves and goblin based. They had stolen a human child to raise as their own. There was a portal to the fairy world via a ring of toadstools. One side of the container was somewhat plain, and was the human world. But behind the toadstool portal was a bridge to the elves and a lush forest. There were goblin guardians hiding in the bushes to stop any humans from getting through.

Another story was of a little cottage hidden in the mountains. This fairy had escaped the human world and cultivated a private hidden paradise in the hard to reach mountains. I used a shelf basket for this, with walls on three sides. I weaved vine like plants through the holes on the side, creating a hidden feel. I had a cute old fashioned cottage, set up a little garden of fairy sized vegetables, and in addition to the single fairy, I filled the area with tiny bunnies. So, this fairy was alone in the mountains surrounded by animals and protective vines.

I think you can get the idea. I just like to tell these stories, and use the plants and fairies to display it. It makes it more fun to show people and tell them about it as well.

Upkeep and Care

We've reached the end my friends. But, your fairy garden can live on with proper care. That's something you can decide though. Maybe you don't mind if your plants don't make it through the winter. If so, that makes this a lot easier.

First you want to think about care during the spring and summer. You should already have the plant where it can get the right amount of sun. You should have an idea of the right amount of watering. Check the health of the plants and the dampness of the soil regularly.

You make think the soil looks dry, but make sure to stick your finger a half inch or so into the dirt. See if the dirt there is damp. If it is, you probably don't need to water. If you notice your plants getting droopy, they probably need water. Another thing to do is test the weight of the pot. If it seems super light, it's probably too dry.

Don't worry about getting it right, you'll figure it out. And you can always get new plants if you don't!

Now, it comes to wintering your fairy gardens. There are a few plants that will survive outside over the winter and come back the next year, they are called perennials. Most of the time you don't end up with these in fairy gardens, with the exception of most mosses.

If you have room and places inside to bring in your plants, you might be able to save a few. I unfortunately don't have much space, I do however have parents that do! I winter many of my plants at my parent's farm. So, consider friends and family that might not mind helping.

If you choose to leave the plants outside, okay with the fact they might not make it through the winter, you still might want to consider keeping your fairy garden pieces safe. Many of them are built for the cold, snow and rain, but some aren't. Plus there is always the chance of them being knocked over and broken in the wind.

I take off most of the fairy pieces each year and pack them up to rebuild next year. This way I get the joy of building them again and again.

The choice here is up to you! I hope that you've enjoyed building your fairy garden with me! Spread the joy and share this with others!

Create the table of contents in Normal manually (as we will set that up using Microsoft Word TOC option).

About The Expert:

Casey Anderson is a woman in her mid-30s who can sometimes remember what it was like to be a child with an overactive imagination. She finds fairies enchanting, miniature gardens invigorating and basically anything tiny delightful. She thinks there's something about small that so often means cute. She's made nearly a hundred fairy gardens. She's entered her fairy gardens in local fairs and won ribbons. Casey also loves the idea of a craft that can be completed without extensive training and skills. She has fun with fairy gardening and loves to instill her passion for it into friends and family members.

HowExpert publishes short 'how to' guides by everyday experts.

Recommended Resources

www.HowExpert.com – Short 'how to' guides on unique topics by everyday experts.

www.HowExpert.com/writers - Write About Your #1 Passion/Knowledge/Experience!

www.HowExpert.com/service - We Can Help Self Publish Your Own Dream Book!

www.HowExpert.com/gardening - Additional resource for Gardening enthusiasts!

Printed in Great Britain
by Amazon